Kenneth Noland

Kenneth Noland

Into the Cool

32 East 57th Street New York January 26 – March 4, 2017

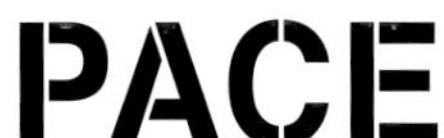

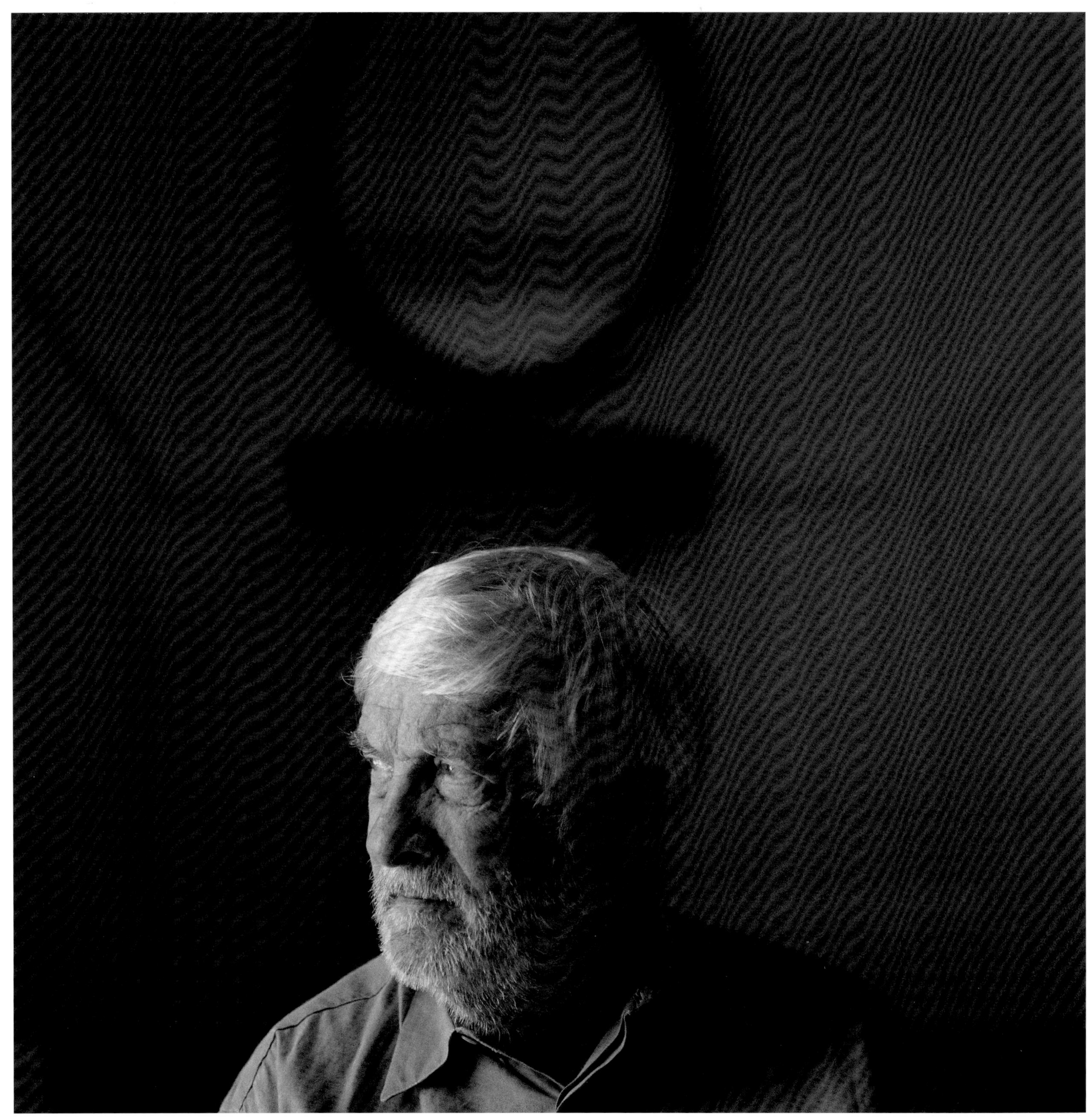

Noland in his studio, Port Clyde, Maine, 2005

Kenneth Noland: The Last Paintings

WILLIAM C. AGEE

In our constant search for the new, we may overlook older artists who have continued to work and to discover new ground. But some of the best art done at any given time has been by artists who did their pioneering art long before. They do not stop. Think only of Monet in the 1920s, who did some of the most glorious painting of that decade. The last paintings done by Kenneth Noland in his long life may well bring a similar surprise. But here they are, fifteen works done in 2006–07, surely among the most compelling paintings made in the twenty-first century. This series is entitled *Into the Cool*, and forms a memorable finale to a monumental body of painting that first appeared some sixty years ago.

They are so different from his work of the preceding twenty-five years that it is fair to consider them a true old-age style, a true *alter Stil*. Old-age art, a fascinating and still little-explored topic, has a long and treasured history and includes Michelangelo, Titian, Rembrandt, Cézanne, Monet, and Matisse, among many others. In most cases, the art became darker, deeper, more mysterious, simpler in Michelangelo's case, more complex in Cézanne's. Only in Matisse do we find a more open, expansive, and even joyful type of art. It is in Matisse, whom Noland termed the greatest artist ever—not just of the twentieth century, but *ever*—that we may locate the mood of Noland's last works.[1]

In his paintings done from 1975 to 2003, Noland used color as density and weight, an all-over fullness, covering the entire canvas, often in irregular shapes, the better, it would seem, to get as much color as possible into any given work. Color had been Noland's goal from the start, color in as many hues, tones, densities, measures, weights, amounts, and transparencies as he could find. Thus, when we enter a room filled with only the morning light and we first see the last paintings, it is as if we are walking into a world of another pictorial and emotional order altogether. We are in a space of vaporous atmospherics that stem from countless washes and touches of soft pastel colors that seem to dance over the surfaces, barely settling in place on the canvas. At points, their material existence may only be affirmed by the light reflecting off the touches of raised gel. Like reflections off the water, or from thin clouds in the sky at sunrise or sunset, the color areas, often independent but at other times mixed into other shapes, seem to flow across, up, down, and back again over the surface. It is as if late in life, new and novel color sequences and passages had been released by a playful and joyful hand. If color bands in Noland's art had once seemed controlled and disciplined, these last paintings bespeak an artist letting color loose, to fend for itself, to go where it might, with the artist no longer controlling so much as looking on with happy appreciation and pleasure.

Light blues, pinks, yellows, and greens are the hues that we mostly see; they seem to have their way; they can touch one another, stand by themselves, be crossed by one shape, then in turn double back and meet another color, fuse with others, or not. The wash, the staining seems so thin, so virtually transparent that we might well wonder how on earth they even stick to the surface. The mood, look, and touch are new.

He never stopped bearing down (as he liked to say) on his quest for a painting based solely on color, as an emotional and physical entity unto itself.[2]

Noland loved the natural world around him, and often his work was based on the landscape, especially in the way edges of water, land, and sky meet and connect.[3] This is really no surprise when we consider how much of abstracting art in America has come from the landscape around us. Think of paintings by Arthur Dove, Jackson Pollock, and Helen Frankenthaler for example, for just a small representation of art based on landscape. In Noland's art, we need only remember *Lunar Episode* (1958), *Heat* (1958), *Noon Afloat* (1962), and *Morning Span* (1964) in his earlier career to see and feel the impress of a given time of day, or weather condition. In his work after 1975, the sense of our presence in the landscape and even cosmos became even more consistent: think of works like *Comet* (1983); *Mysteries: Toward East Light* (2002); or *Reflections: Starry Nights* (2003). In all, even in those, in which the hues are softer, the color is solid, well-defined, palpable in its (and our) presence. These are all wonderful paintings and Noland might well have continued in this vein with great success. But that was not his way. To the end, he pushed his explorations, like a scientist, always seeking ever-newer ways of using color.

But make no mistake; these paintings, although lyrical in tone, have their own complexity, and even their own history. In fact, they raise more questions and hold more mysteries, at least for this writer, than perhaps any other aspect of his art. His approach always seemed to be one of seeking and asking himself new questions: what if I do this? What might happen if I tried that? He loved to turn a painting around to see how it might work with a new orientation. It was an attitude of constant experimentation, refusing to settle into a given mode. The world, and the world of color, was too vast to allow for that. The last paintings and their pastel hues seem free and easy, but these works have other, multiple surprises for us.

Several of them have been painted and drawn on the verso side as well as the front. It is as if Noland had decided to keep going, in his own private world, unavailable to the viewers, except in the back room. Often these areas of paint, strong on the back, seep through the canvas and create visible formations on the front. These same colors are now changed into almost ghostly apparitions, as seen in *Into the Cool No. 4* (p. 16). The back is bright and strong, really a separate painting, that may remind us of Noland's early Abstract Expressionist works, hardly known today; but it becomes something else altogether on the front, changed as if by a magical trick. It is another way of making the color coeval with the support, always the objective from the mid-1950s on. He seems to have asked himself a simple question: If we can stain paint from the front, why not from the back as well? The result can seem as if he were actually painting with watercolor, in the spirit of other Maine artists such as Winslow Homer and John Marin. A master can paint any type of picture.

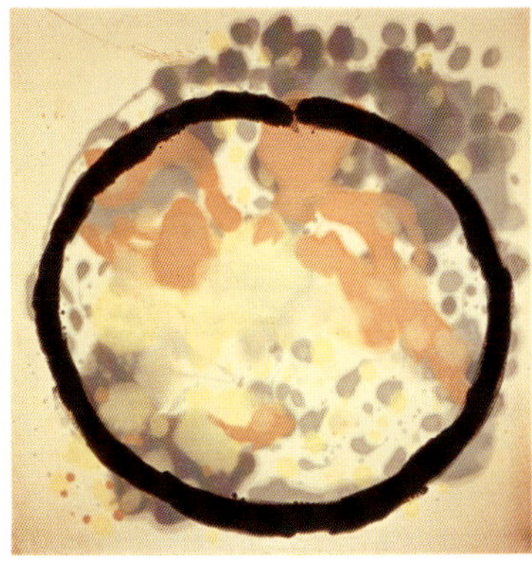

fig. 1 *Globe*, 1956
oil on canvas, 60 x 60"
Collection of Cornelia Reis

It seems to me that in these paintings, he was going back to his roots, both in his own early works and in the work of artists he had respected and learned from. The very first painting that included a discrete circle, *Globe* of 1956 (fig. 1), was formed by soft, even faint blotches of paint which, though not stained from the back, certainly creates the impression that they were. Could the last paintings be an effort to connect with his beginnings? (This writer has sought that in his own work.) Could he go back and see what might have happened if he had continued in the vein of diffused paint areas? Working on both sides was made explicit in *Back and Front* (fig. 2), a concentric circle painting from 1960, and while it may look incomplete on both sides, the artist considered it finished. The images on both recto and verso are made complete by the painting on both sides of the unprimed canvas. It is as if Noland wanted us to see *inside* the hues, to get into the material substance of the paint itself. The same material, the same hue becomes two different hues, with varying shades and tones. We see from the front only half, in effect, of the

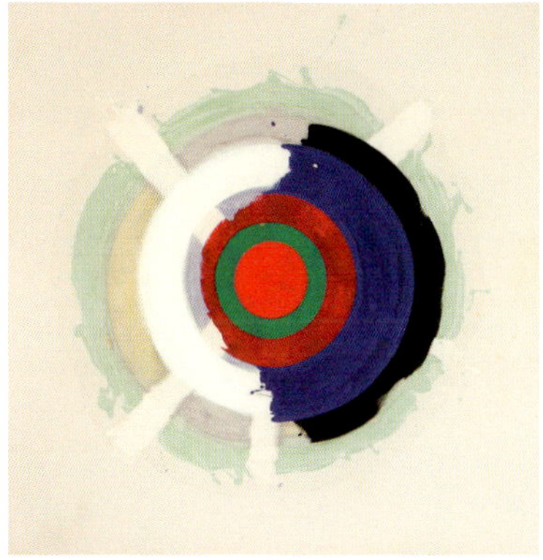

fig. 2 *Back and Front*, 1960
acrylic on canvas, 69 x 69"
Private collection

applied paint—only a suggestion of what it started as. For those who think color painting is direct and easy, these late paintings will demand that we rethink the whole process. They offer a lesson into the complexity of making a painting, of painting itself, letting us see for ourselves behind the scenes, grappling with all that goes into making a work of art.

The title *Into the Cool* refers to the jazz of Gil Evans, whom Noland, always a jazz buff, particularly admired, and whose music he was listening to at the time he did the series. Noland supported Evans's artistic endeavors: he supplied him with instruments, recorded some of Evans's performances, and financed one of his albums.[4] Evans is thought to be one of the musicians responsible for the birth of the cool sound in the late 1940s. But Evans's famous album of 1960 was actually entitled *Out of the Cool*. Why did Noland reverse it? Can we say Noland wanted to keep the work *within* the scope of the harmonies of the Evans album? It can be risky to equate music and painting too literally, but when we listen to Evans it certainly does evoke the atmosphere, soft and mellow, much like the last paintings. Cool also signifies fashionable, stylish, chic, up-to-the-minute, sophisticated, hip, big, happening, groovy, being in a state of pleasure, doing something at its best. All can be said to evoke how Noland must have felt about these paintings.

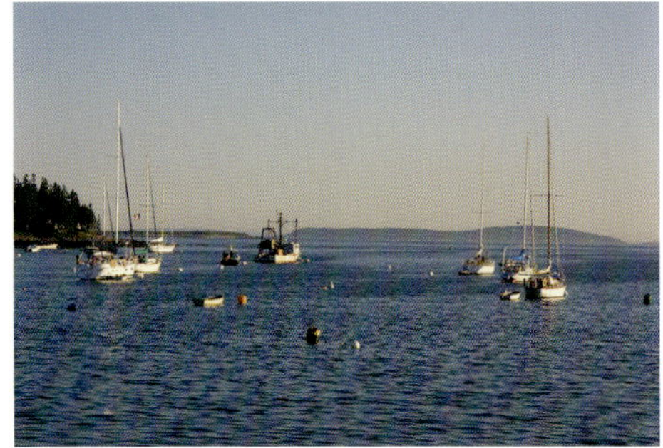
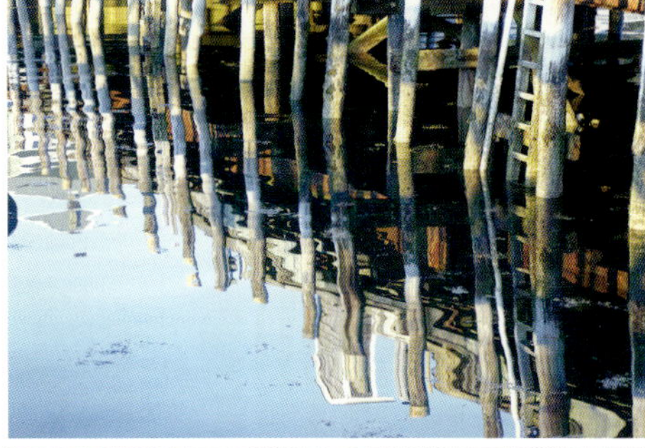
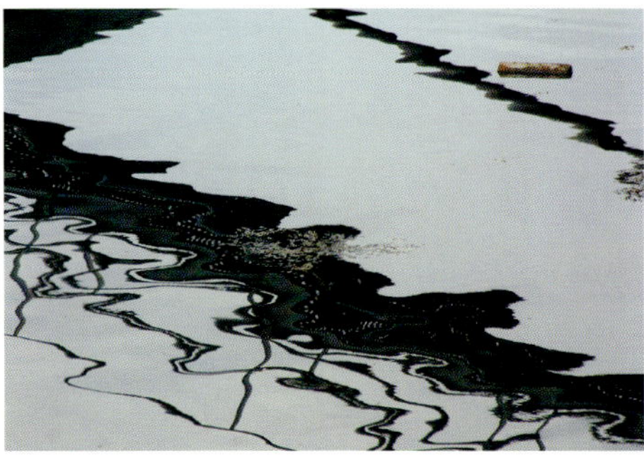

fig. 3 Photographs taken by Kenneth Noland, Port Clyde, Maine, 2001

Noland was an avid photographer, recording his natural surroundings and the effects of weather on the sky and water around him, first in California, then in Port Clyde, Maine, where he had settled in 2002. The light there affects everything, it is in constant play and dominates in his photographs (fig. 3). I feel we can be certain that the play of light on and in the sky and water is at the heart of the last works. The yellows, reds, blues, greens all bring to mind the movements of the natural world, the sun, sky, land, and water, all in constant motion, always changing. We find the landscape in Pollock (*Autumn Rhythm*, 1950) and of course in Frankenthaler (*Mountains and Sea*, 1952; fig. 4), the inventor of direct stain painting, and surely Noland is paying homage to them, at least in part, in these paintings. The flow of organic shapes in these last Nolands will recall them both. Staining from the back was done by James Brooks in the early 1950s; whether Noland knew about Brooks's paintings is open to question, but here Noland has taken the practice to a full working methodology. The pale and soft colors have a feminine feel to them, and in this he may be pointing to Frankenthaler in another way. Certainly, his visit to her studio in 1953 set him on the way to his own mature art. If these last works are abstractions of the sky, of the atmosphere around us, as I am certain they are, one cannot help but recall Alfred Stieglitz's famous photographs of clouds and sky, his *Equivalents* series.

Noland also returned to his original practice of working on the floor. He gave up the eccentric shapes of his paintings of the last twenty-five years and returned to the standard rectangular shape of his earlier paintings. The paintings vary in size—the smallest is 51 x 48 inches and the largest is 98 x 98 inches, a practice that ensured he could work these paintings in various sizes and internal scales, all factors that help determine the impact color will have on us. There are sub-series within the group as well. *Nos.* 2, 3, and 4 are large, telling us that Noland wasted no time in taking these paintings to their fullest, all the way out right at the start; the forms are fairly broad and regular and look as if they had been done with a brush or sponge. *No.* 2 has a thin circle coming through on the front, applied from the back to keep it discrete. The circle takes us back to his first paintings, but in a much different way. It barely holds the color together in a rough circle; it doesn't need to do more because the color is self-organizing, encircling itself by its own rotation. Noland is here telling us what he had told us from the beginning: in the paintings of the 1950s and later, the circle was not an arbitrarily applied design formula but was an updated, abstract distillation of the tendency of most modern (and Renaissance) paintings to seek the center. Color and forms around the edges gather in the composition like bookends, pulling the painting together toward the center, forcing our eye to the center.

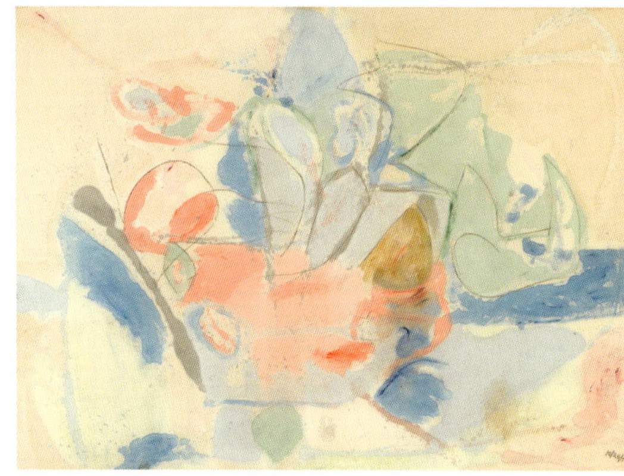

fig. 4 Helen Frankenthaler
Mountains and Sea, 1952
oil and charcoal on canvas, 86 ⅜ x 117 ¼"
Helen Frankenthaler Foundation,
on loan to the National Gallery of Art, Washington, D.C.

Noland spoke at length about this effect, citing in particular Pollock's *Autumn Rhythm* (The Metropolitan Museum of Art) and Cézanne's *Grand Bathers* (Philadelphia Museum of Art).[5] Once we see this we will understand Noland's art far better. Indeed, a book has been written on the power of the center.[6] By center, Noland meant the location on the canvas, which enabled the viewer to gain kinetic balance when facing the painting. In turn, this would enable us to find our own center, our own locus of stability, physically and emotionally. From this we are prepared to experience the painting as a single expressive entity, a total expressive whole in which the form equals what it represents: a wave is that form, it is not depicted. It is no accident that when we are out of sorts, or upset, we say "I have to get myself centered, I have to find my center." The unity in the painting equals the unity and balance we find in ourselves; we are one with ourselves, the work, and the world.

The circle is stronger and clearer in *No.* 3 (p. 14); here and in *No.* 2 (p. 12), the soft pastels are made more tangible by hits of gel. *No.* 4 as described above has the most dramatically different front and back; strongest on the back, faintest on the front. To counter this, the circle is decisively drawn then augmented by a white aurora, making a most beautiful effect.

Nos. 5 and 6 (pp. 18, 20) continue in the direction of faint hues, almost to the point where Noland appeared ready to paint himself out of the picture. The color, the paint, seems to float; the hits of gel keep the paint on the surface, to give us points of orientation on this wispy surface.

Having tested the proposition of how little paint he could use, he moved to a brighter, stronger surface in No. 7 (p. 22), in which there are more straight lines, a more material surface with areas of gel, applied in small sharp staccato hits. In No. 9 (p. 26), Noland goes back to larger shapes. He lets color and paint actually flow, then contrasts this with discrete shapes that travel their own course so there are two different internal movements. It is painted from the back where the formations are especially strong and may remind us of geometric forms, perhaps a nod to his earlier painting, and perhaps even a thank you to Ilya Bolotowsky, his teacher at Black Mountain College. He uses drips and splatters, as he had in his early circle paintings. This was new for him, a new freedom we may say. He follows this pattern in No. 10 (p. 28) but adds more small hits of gel. In each, the circle traverses a path through, in, and over the color. No. 11 (p. 30) follows the same pattern but the shapes are more pronounced and are punctuated by a strong concentration of blue and green at dead center.

Noland pushed color to the edges in No. 13 (p. 34), filling the canvas in a way he had not earlier in the series. Too much he seemed to say, for in No. 15 (p. 36) the circumference is tightened, pulled in, and the color is minimized. Color in No. 16 (p. 38) is allowed to float across the circle to some degree. In No. 18 (p. 42) the hues are softer and gentler in ways found in only a few others. The circle becomes smaller and sharper as if to keep us focused amid this hazy atmosphere. Then, in what I read as Noland's finale, a painting entitled *Burst* (p. 46), he combined all he had discovered over the course of the series: it is a painting of perfect pitch, a fusion of emphatic color at right center to barely discernible at left and center bottom; an in and out weaving of pinks and blues; quasi-geometric shapes with an amorphous bleeding of the hues with a touch of mastery that certifies Noland's genius. Then, almost as an exit, a single line from the bottom of the circle to the lower edge takes us quietly out of the gentle pictorial turmoil of the painting. The painting may refer to Adolph Gottlieb's paintings after 1958, in which circles of another kind were prominent, works we know Noland respected, but *Burst* is Noland's alone. It is a strong but quiet painting, not spectacular, but it induces a meditative, contemplative aura that invites us into a private dialogue with the art, the artist, and the world around us. That has always been the way of the best art.

1 My quotations come from extensive conversations with Noland c. 1991–93. See my catalogues on the artist: *Kenneth Noland: The Circle Paintings*, exh. cat. (Houston: Museum of Fine Arts, 1993) and *Kenneth Noland: Painting 1975–2003*, exh. cat. (New York: Pace Gallery, 2014). For other in-depth discussions on the artist, see also Diane Waldman, *Kenneth Noland: A Retrospective*, exh. cat. (New York: Solomon R. Guggenheim Museum, 1977); Karen Wilkin, *Kenneth Noland* (New York: Rizzoli, 1990).

2 See my essays "Kenneth Noland: The Circle Paintings, 1956–1963" and "Noland Post-1976: Color, Light, the Cosmos" in, respectively, *Kenneth Noland: The Circle Paintings* and *Kenneth Noland: Paintings 1975–2003*.

3 Interview with Kenneth Noland conducted by Paul Cummings for the Archives of American Art, October 9–December 21, 1971.

4 For more on Evans and Noland, see Stephanie Stein Crease, *Gil Evans: Out of the Cool: His Life and Music* (Chicago: A Cappella, 2003), 282.

5 Conversation between Kenneth Noland and William C. Agee, early 1990s.

6 Rudolf Arnheim, *The Power of the Center: A Study of Composition in the Visual Arts* (Berkeley: University of California Pres, 1982).

Into the Cool No. 2 2006 acrylic on canvas 98 x 98"

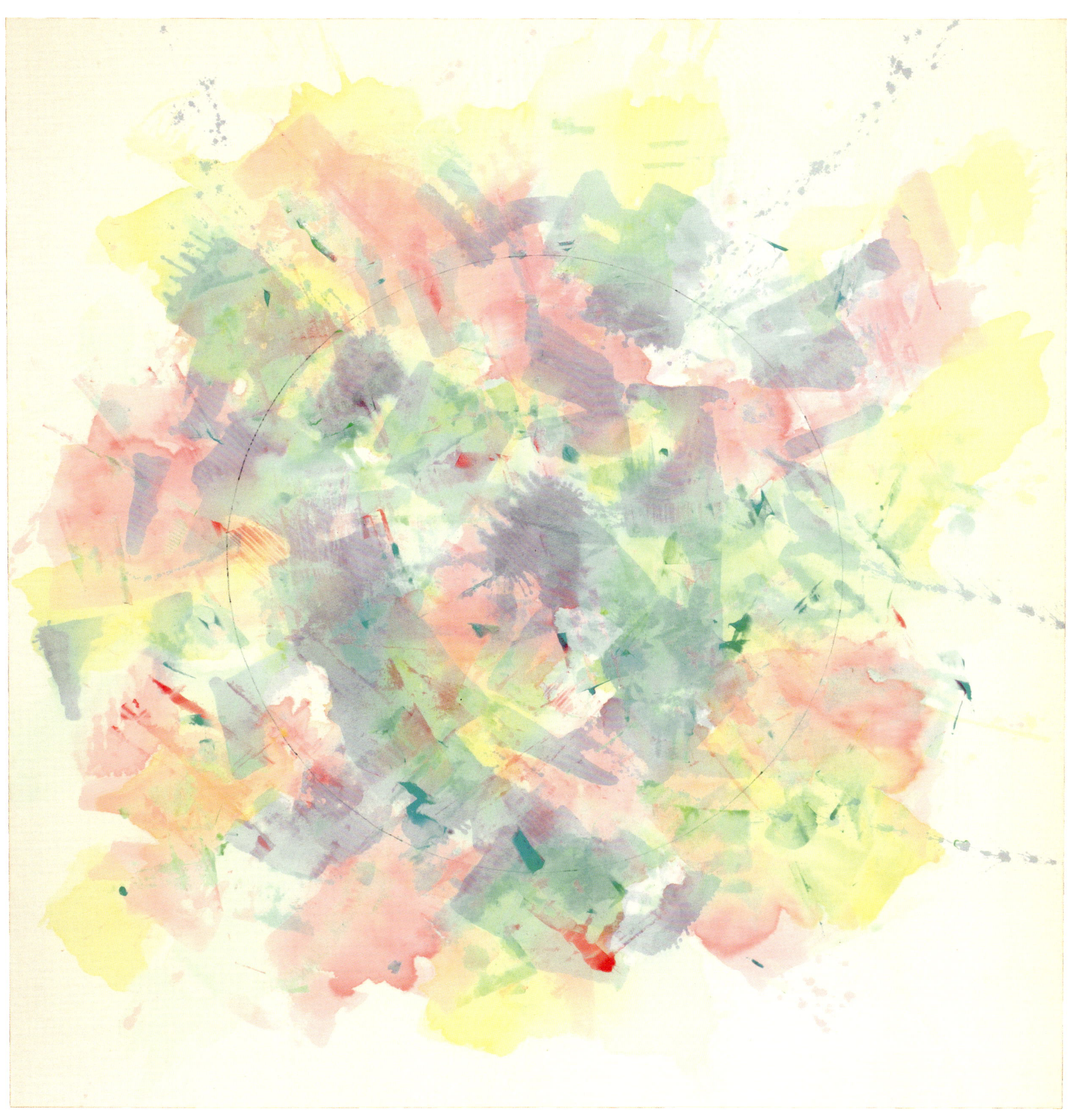

Into the Cool No. 3 2006 acrylic on canvas 68 3/16 x 68 3/16"

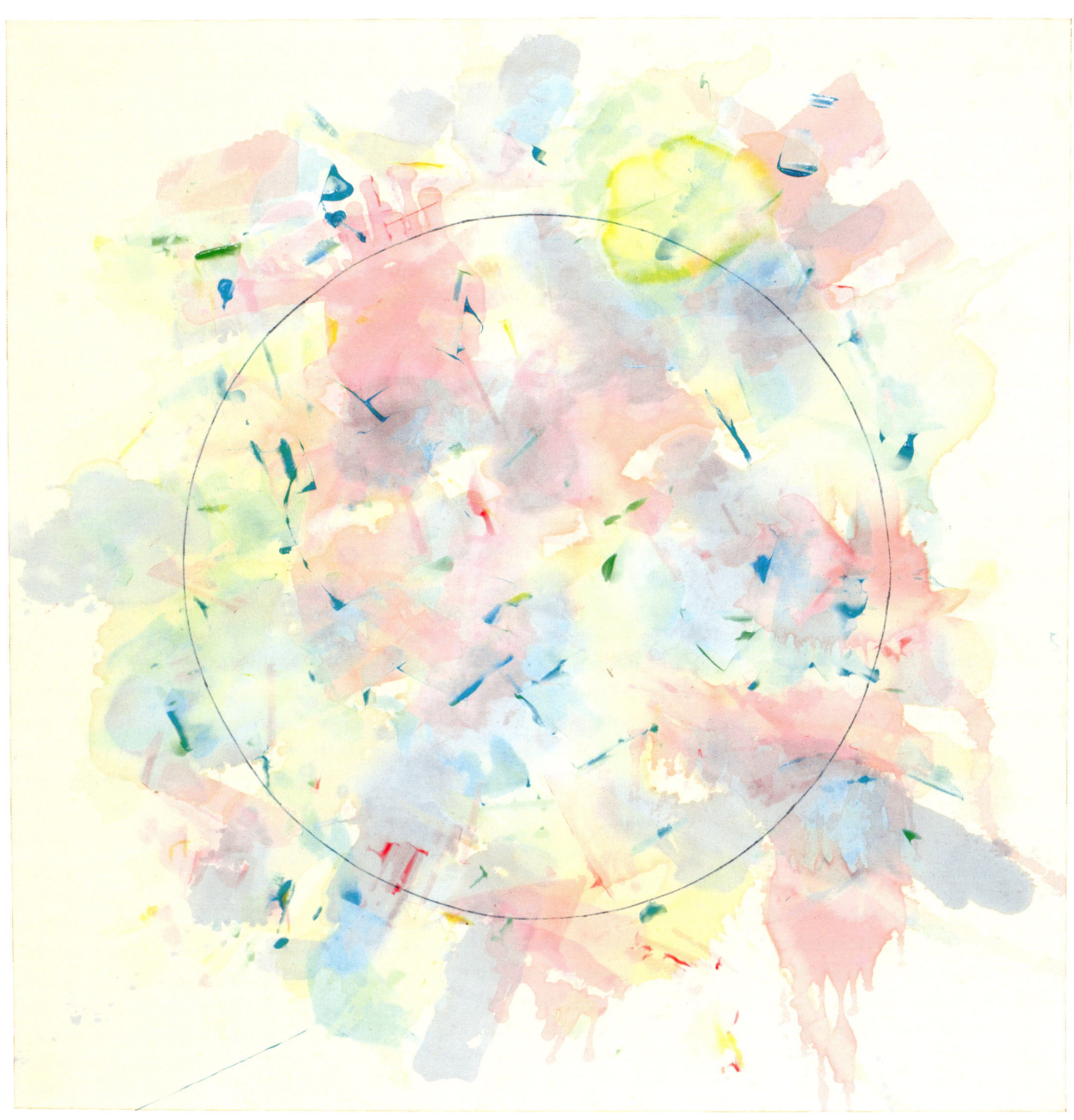

Into the Cool No. 4 2006 acrylic on canvas 80 x 80"

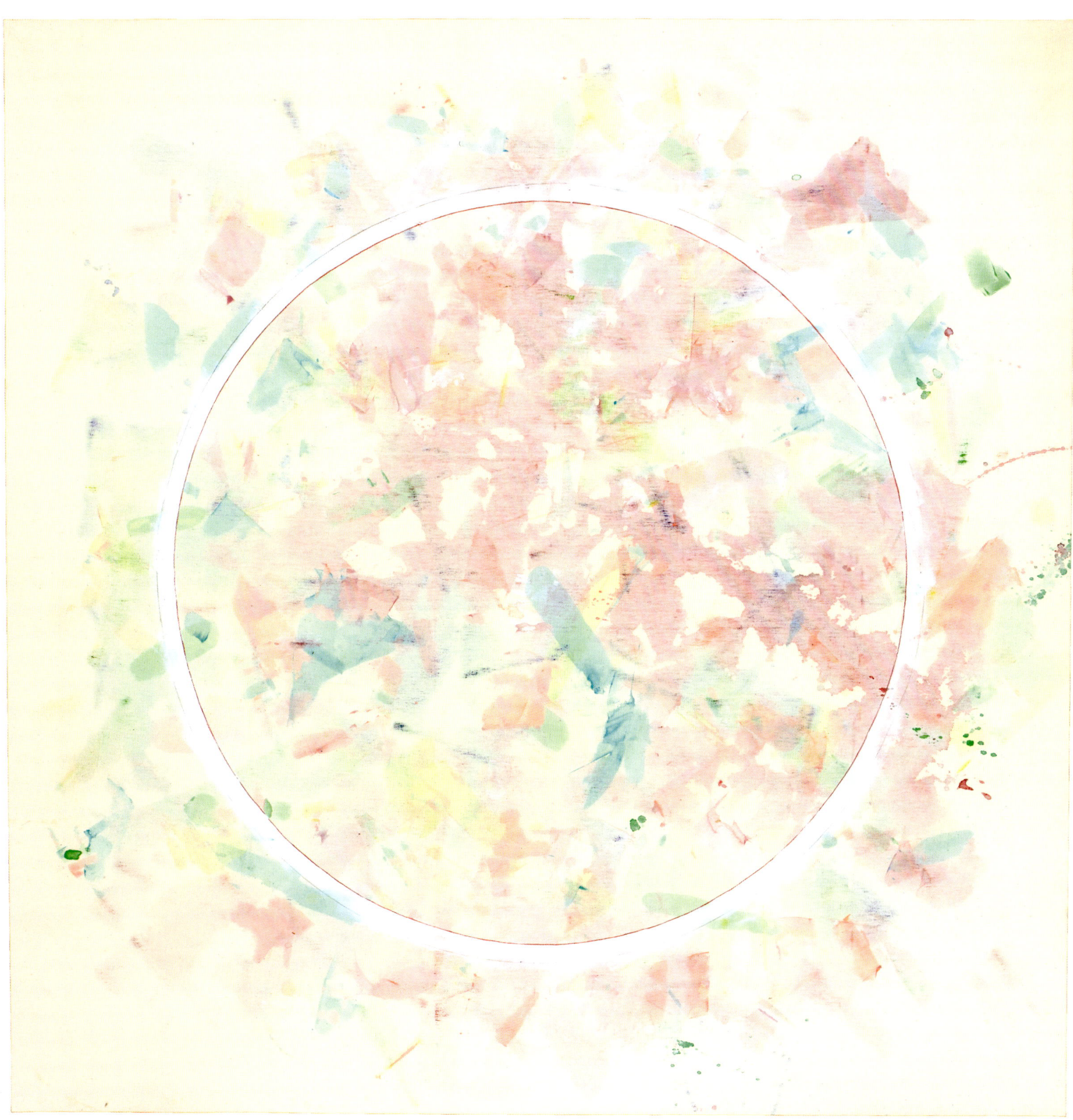

Into the Cool No. 5 2006 acrylic on canvas 80 x 80"

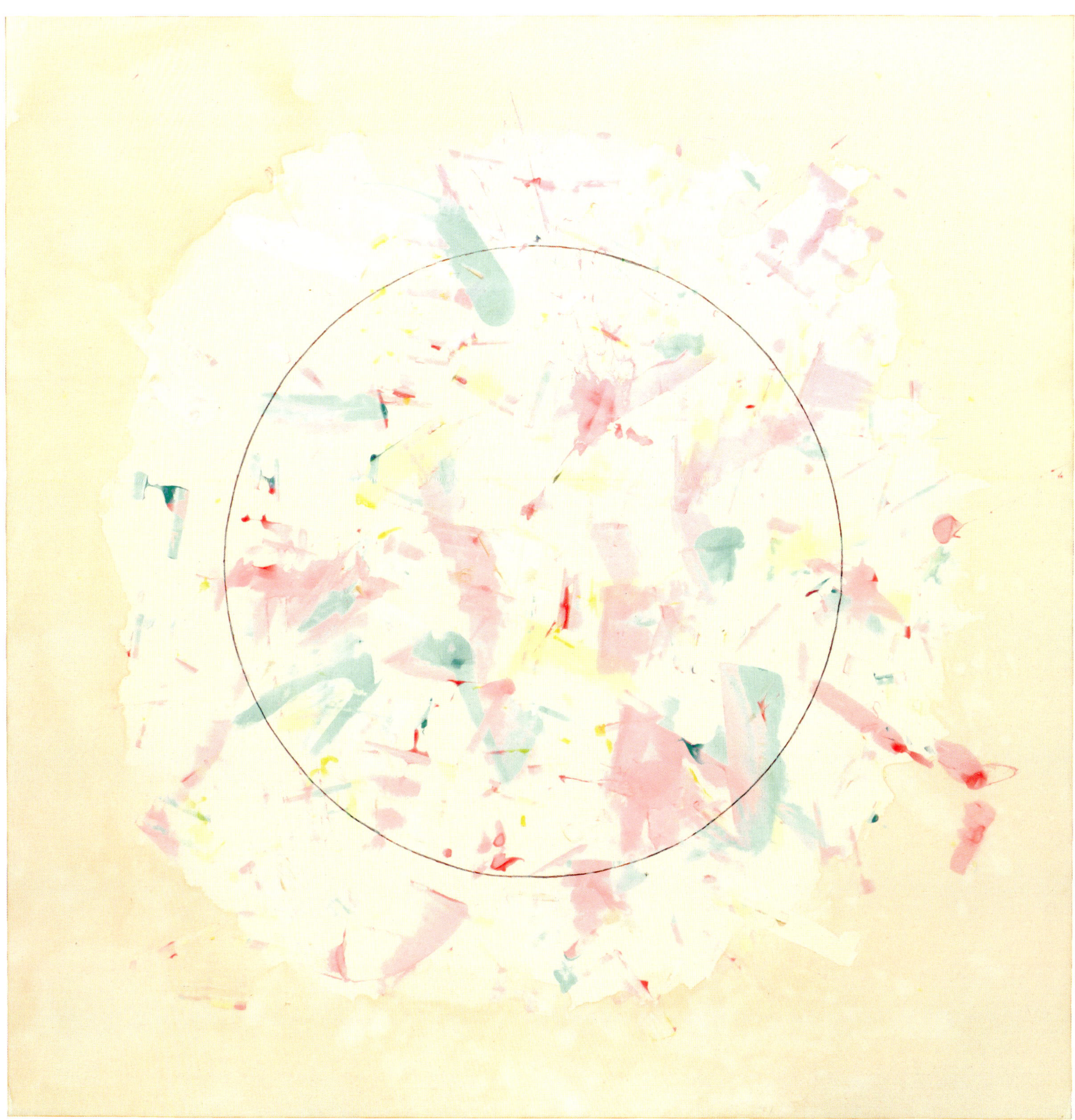

Into the Cool No. 6 2006 acrylic on canvas 80 x 80"

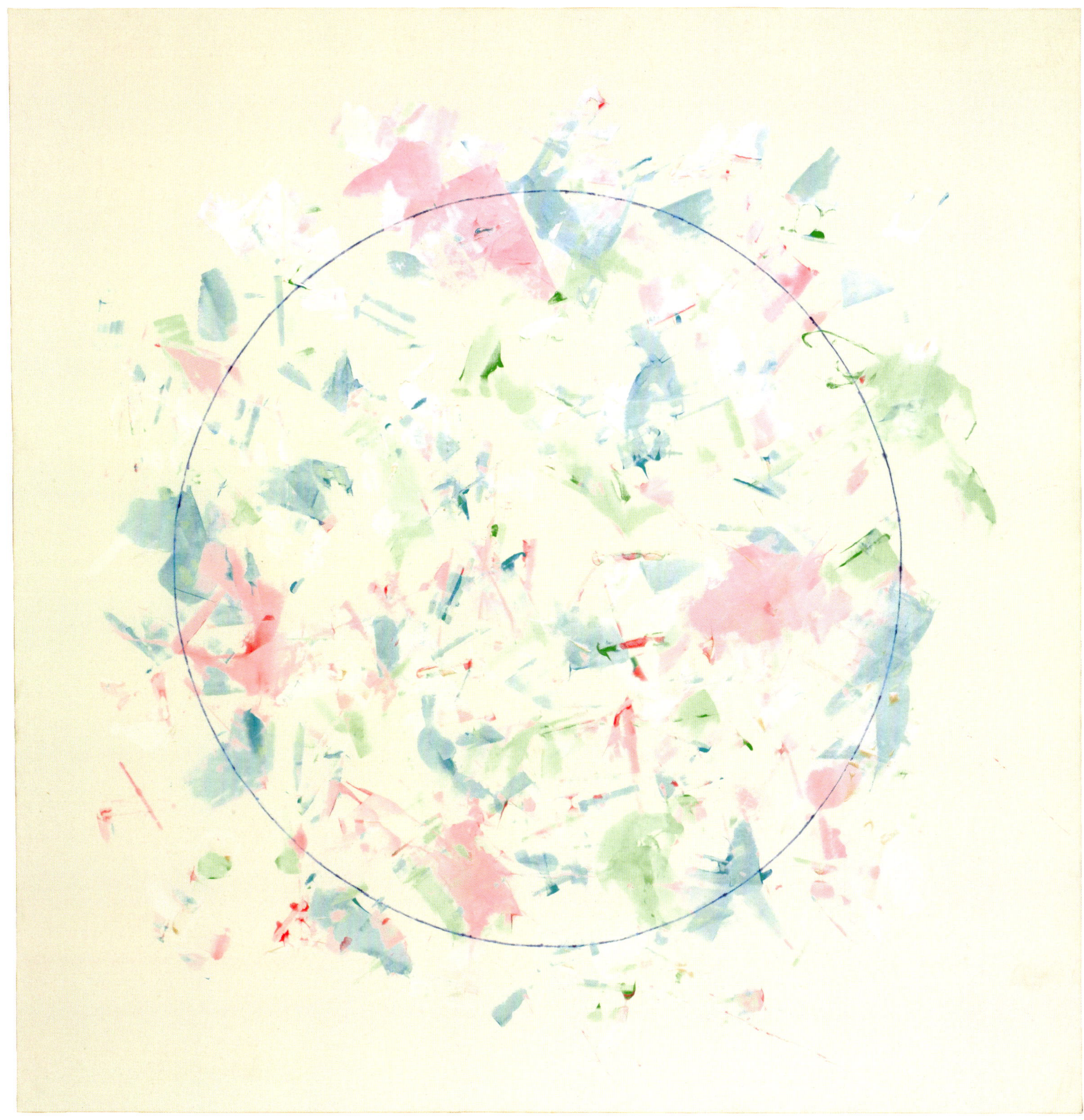

Into the Cool No. 7 2006 acrylic on canvas 80 ½ x 80 ½"

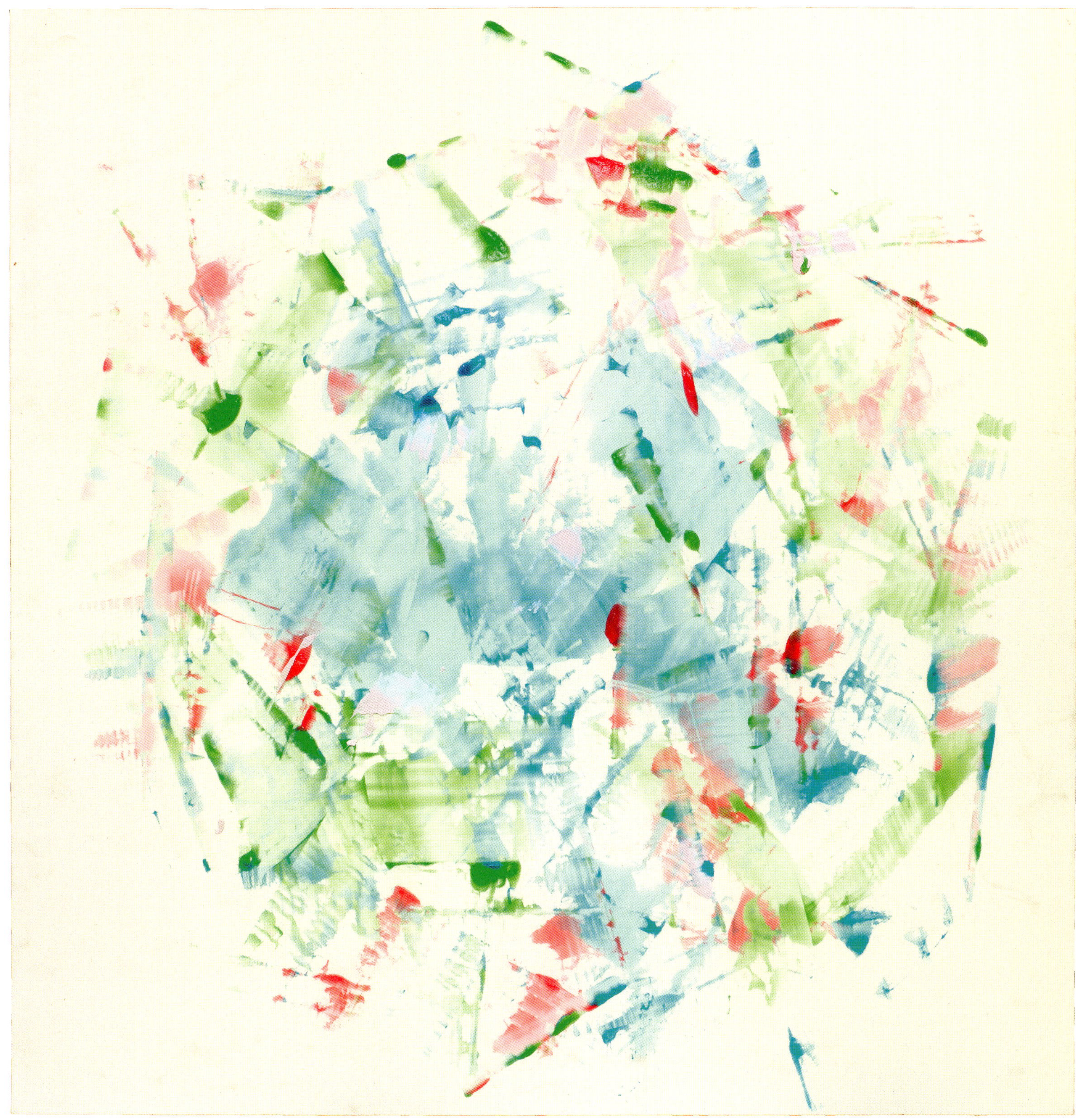

Into the Cool No. 8 2006 acrylic on canvas 80 x 80"

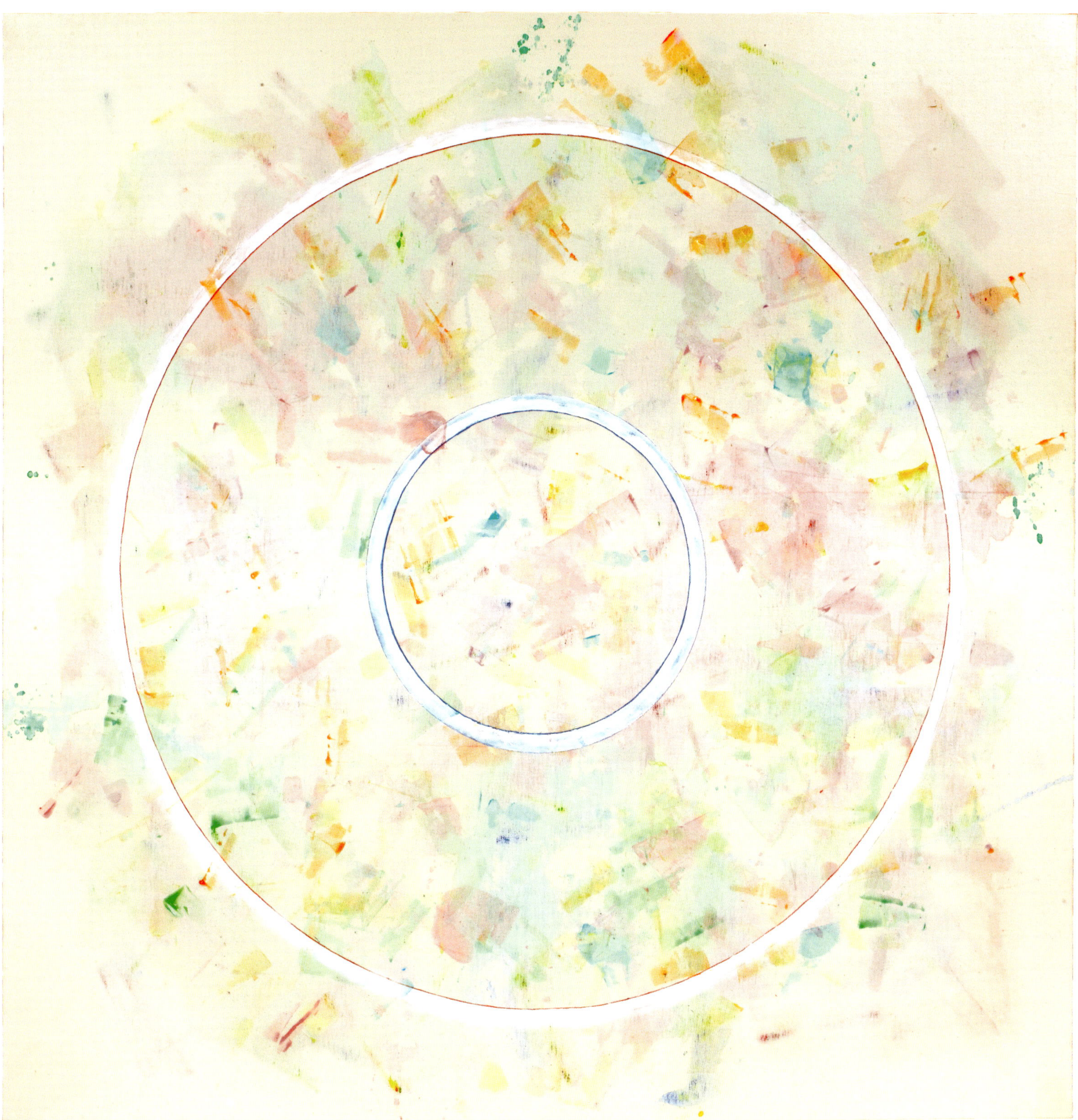

Into the Cool No. 9 2006 acrylic on canvas 66 x 64"

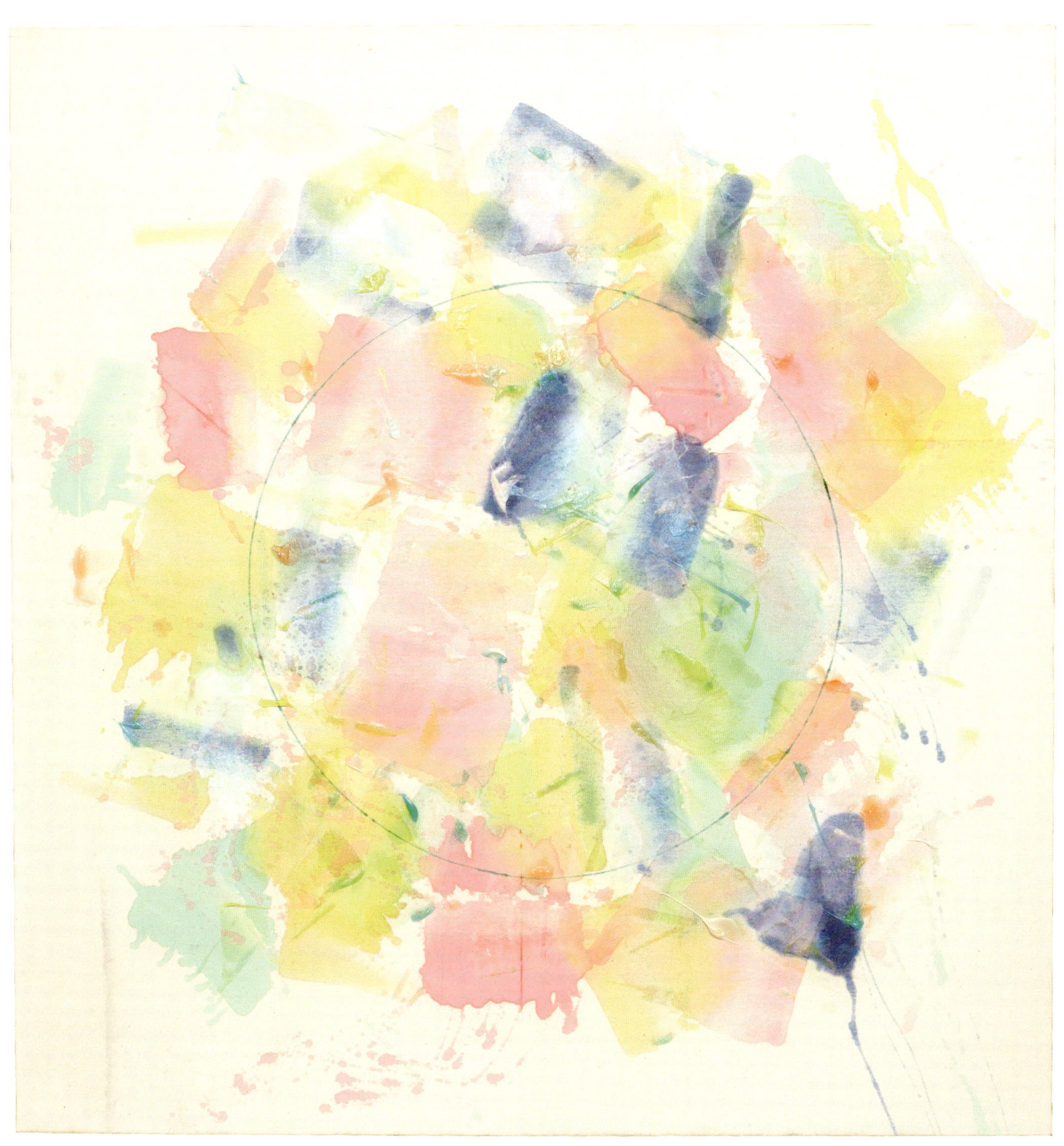

Into the Cool No. 10 2006 acrylic on canvas 67 x 63"

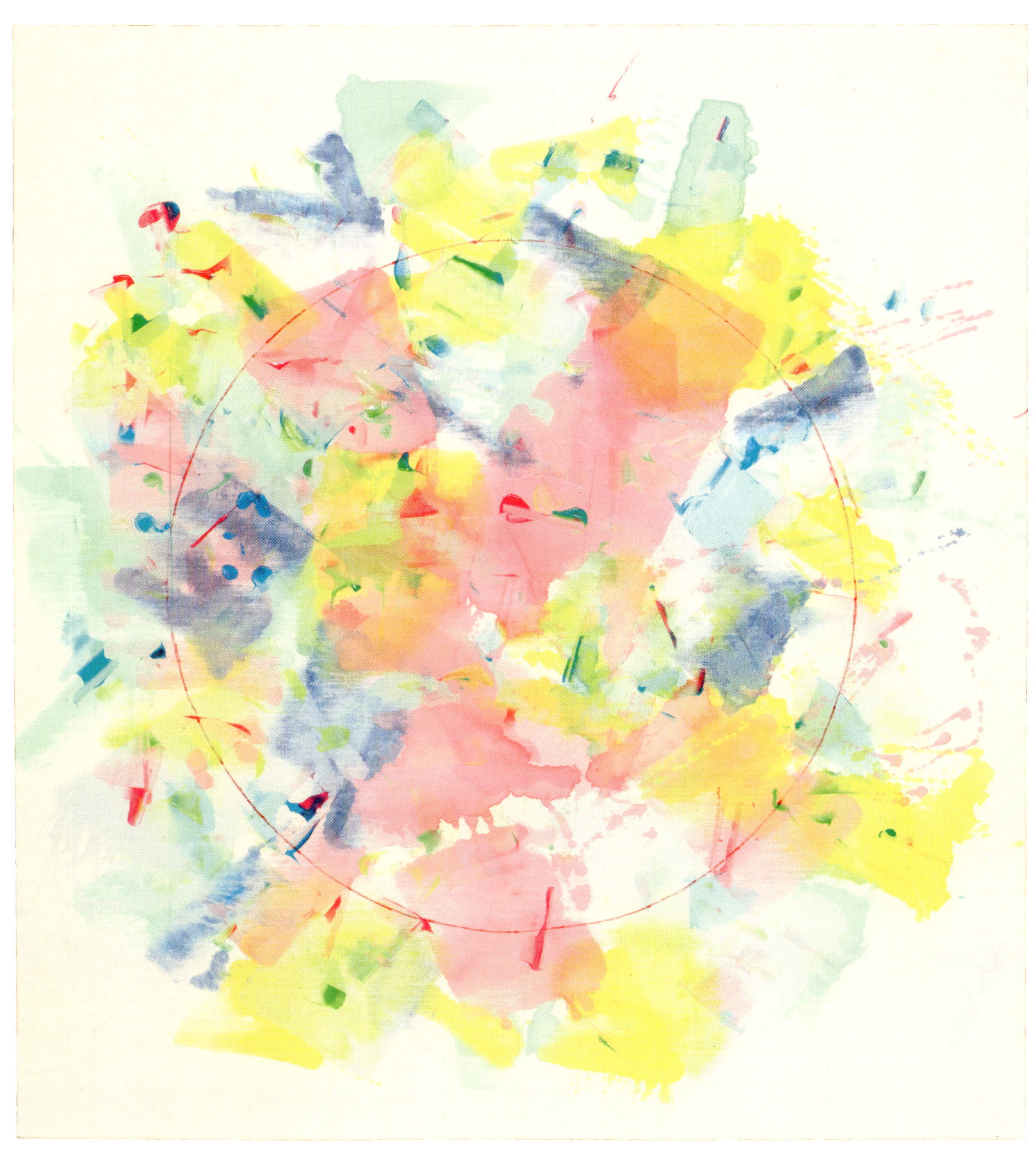

Into the Cool No. 11 2006 acrylic on canvas 65 x 60"

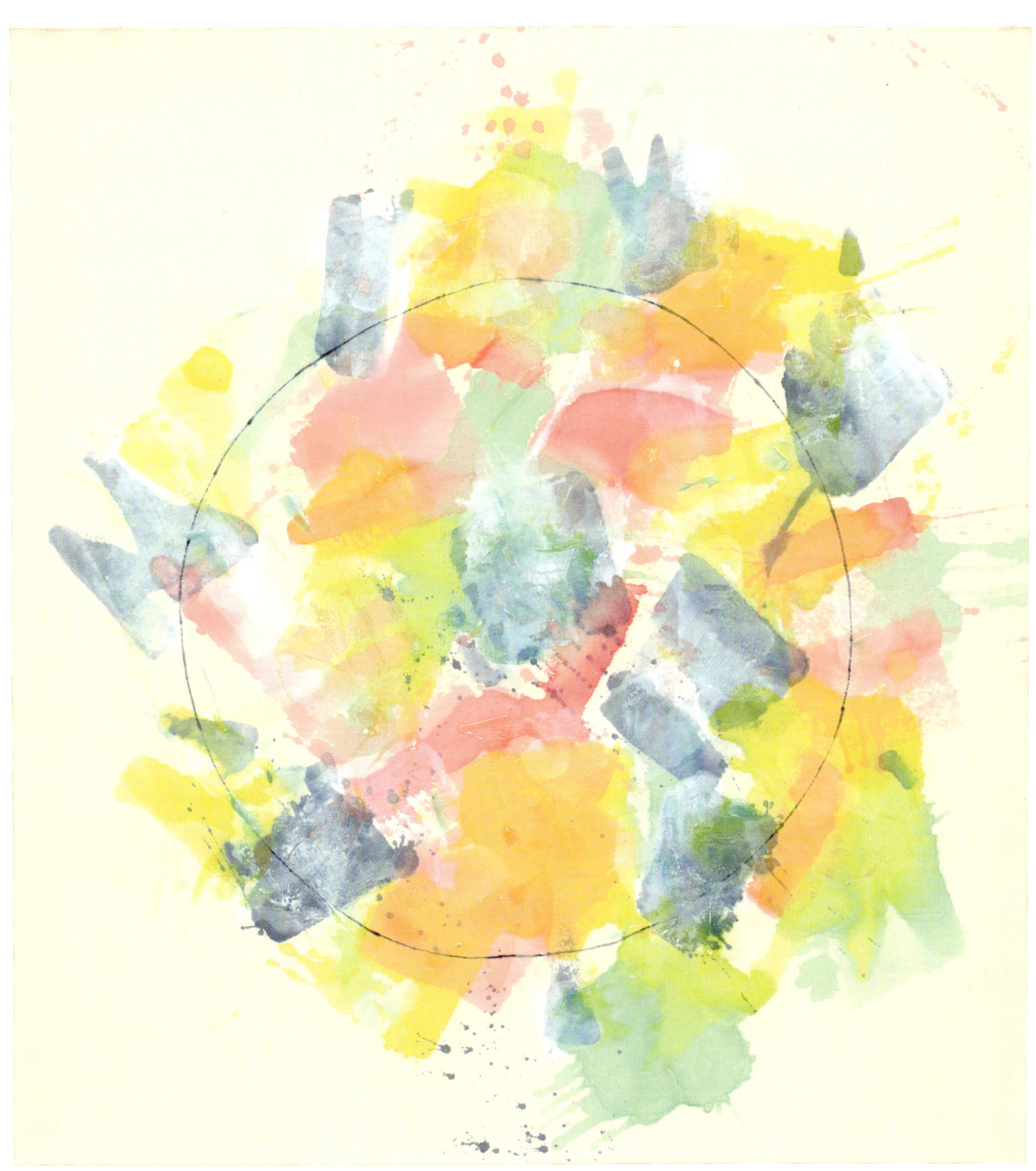

Into the Cool No. 12 2006 acrylic on canvas 51 x 48"

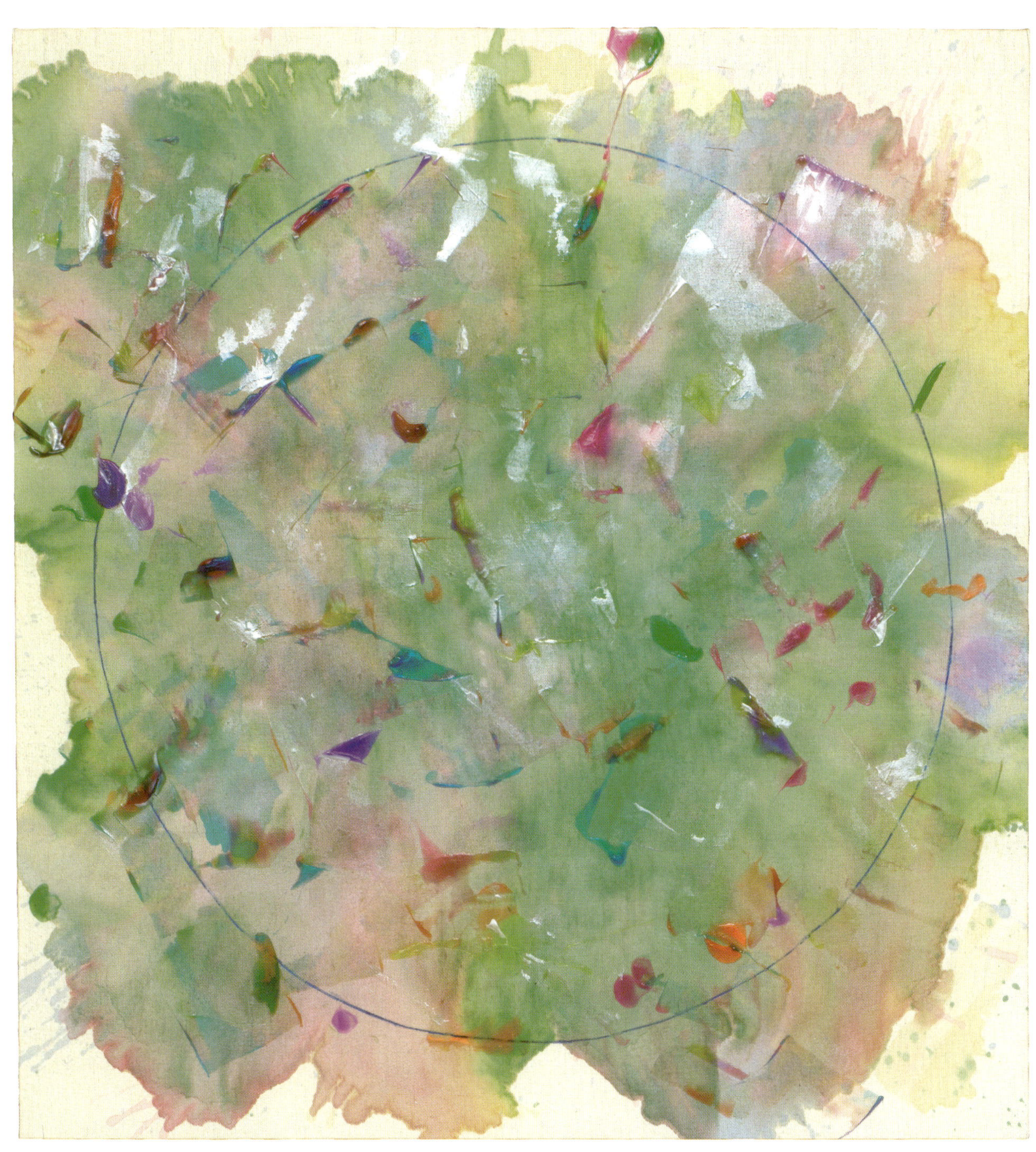

Into the Cool No. 13 2006 acrylic on canvas 84 x 61 ½"

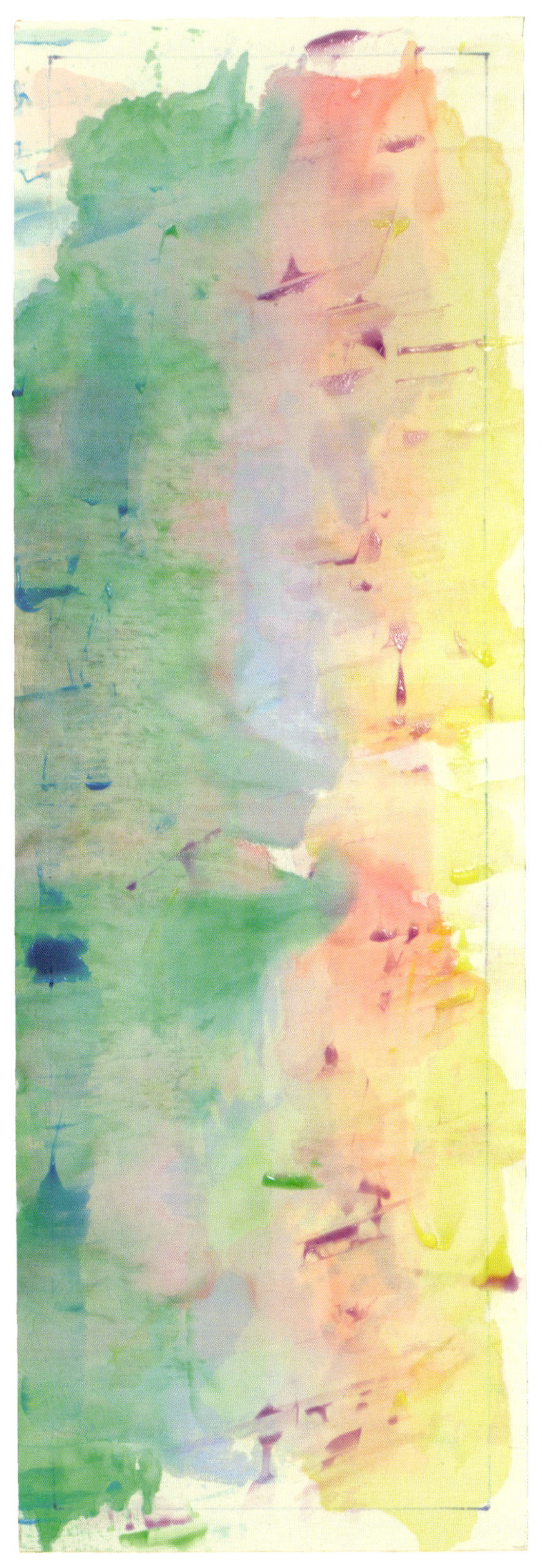
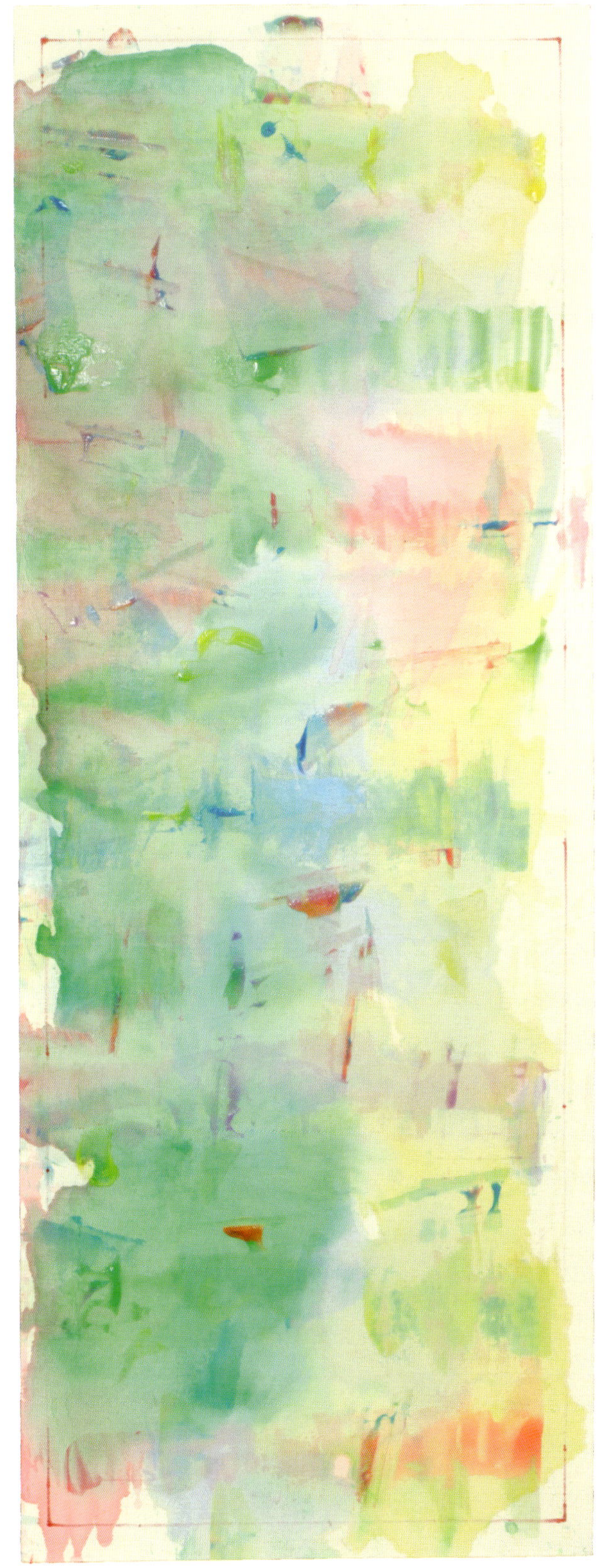

Into the Cool No. 15 2006 acrylic on canvas 62 x 62"

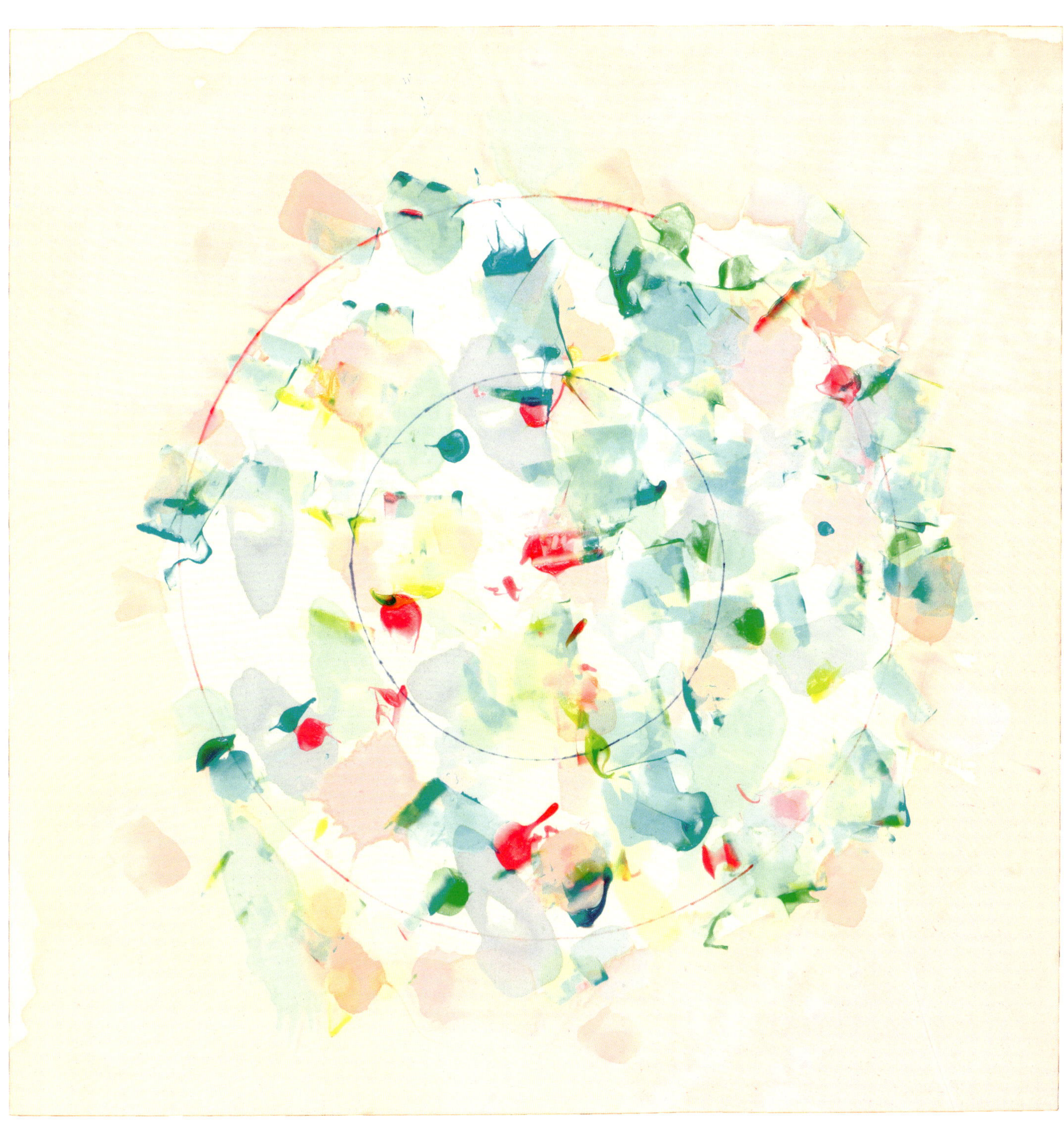

Into the Cool No. 16 2006 acrylic on canvas 55 x 55"

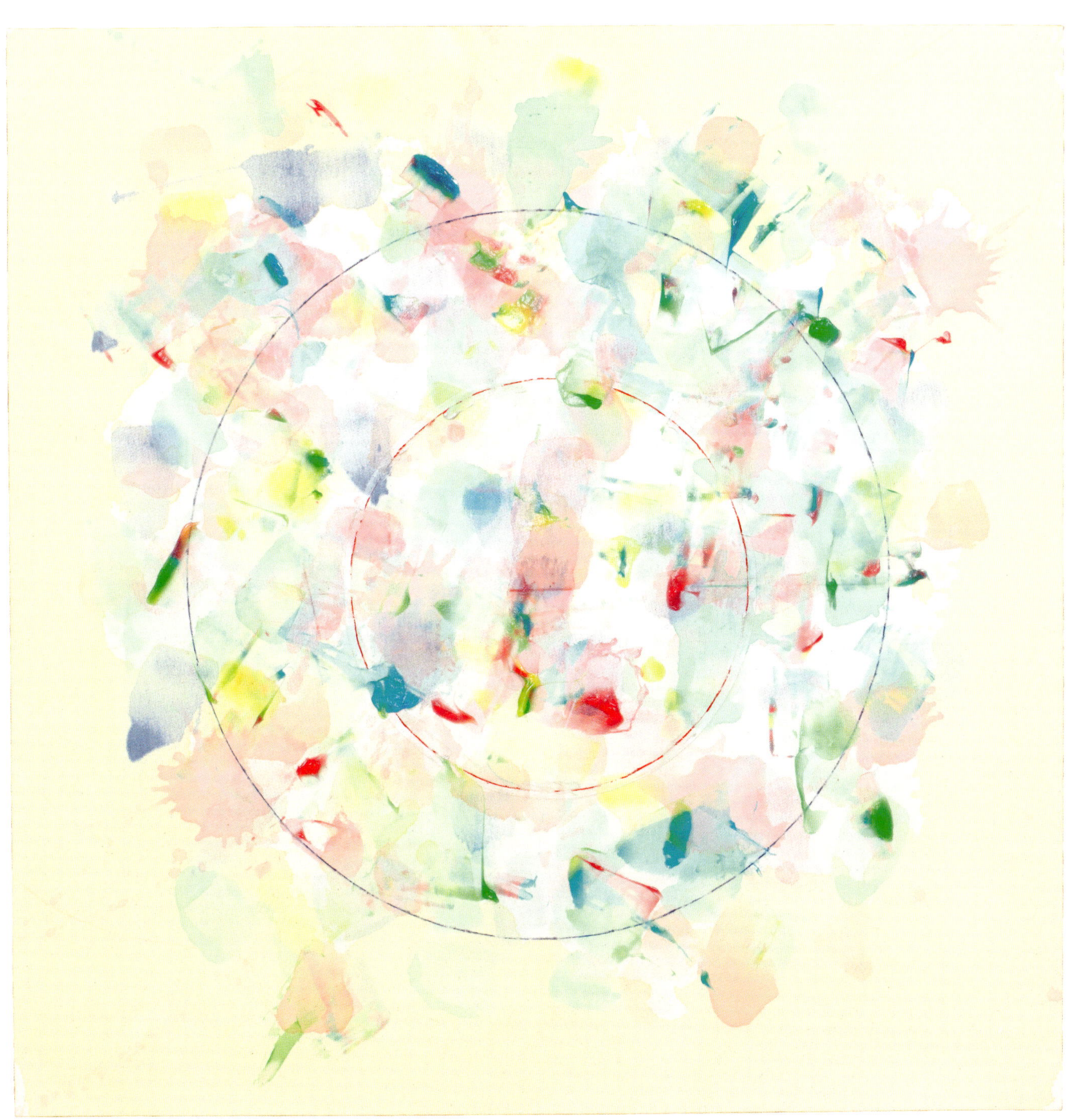

Into the Cool No. 17 2006 acrylic on canvas 60 x 60"

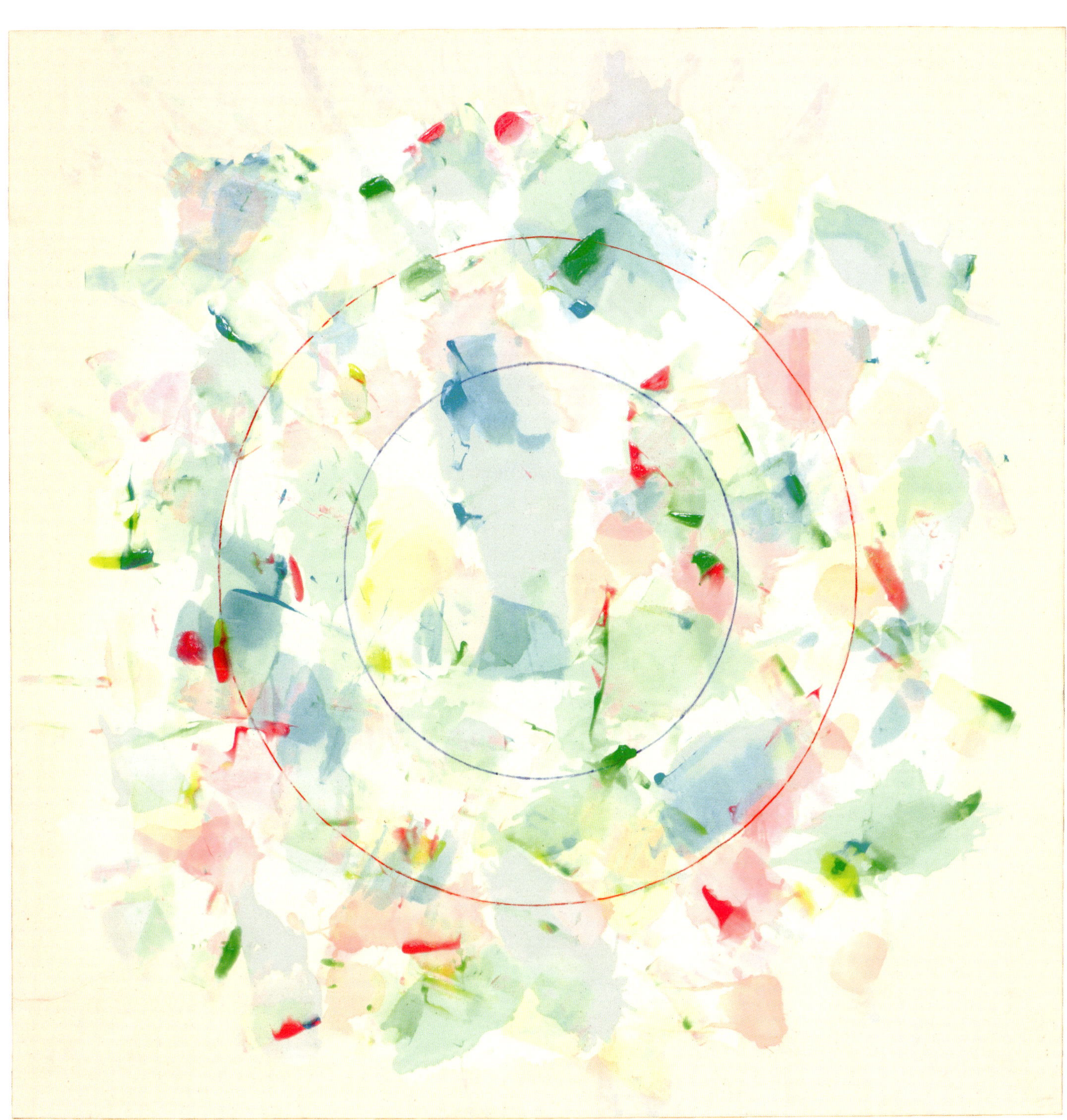

Into the Cool No. 18 2006 acrylic on canvas 62 x 62"

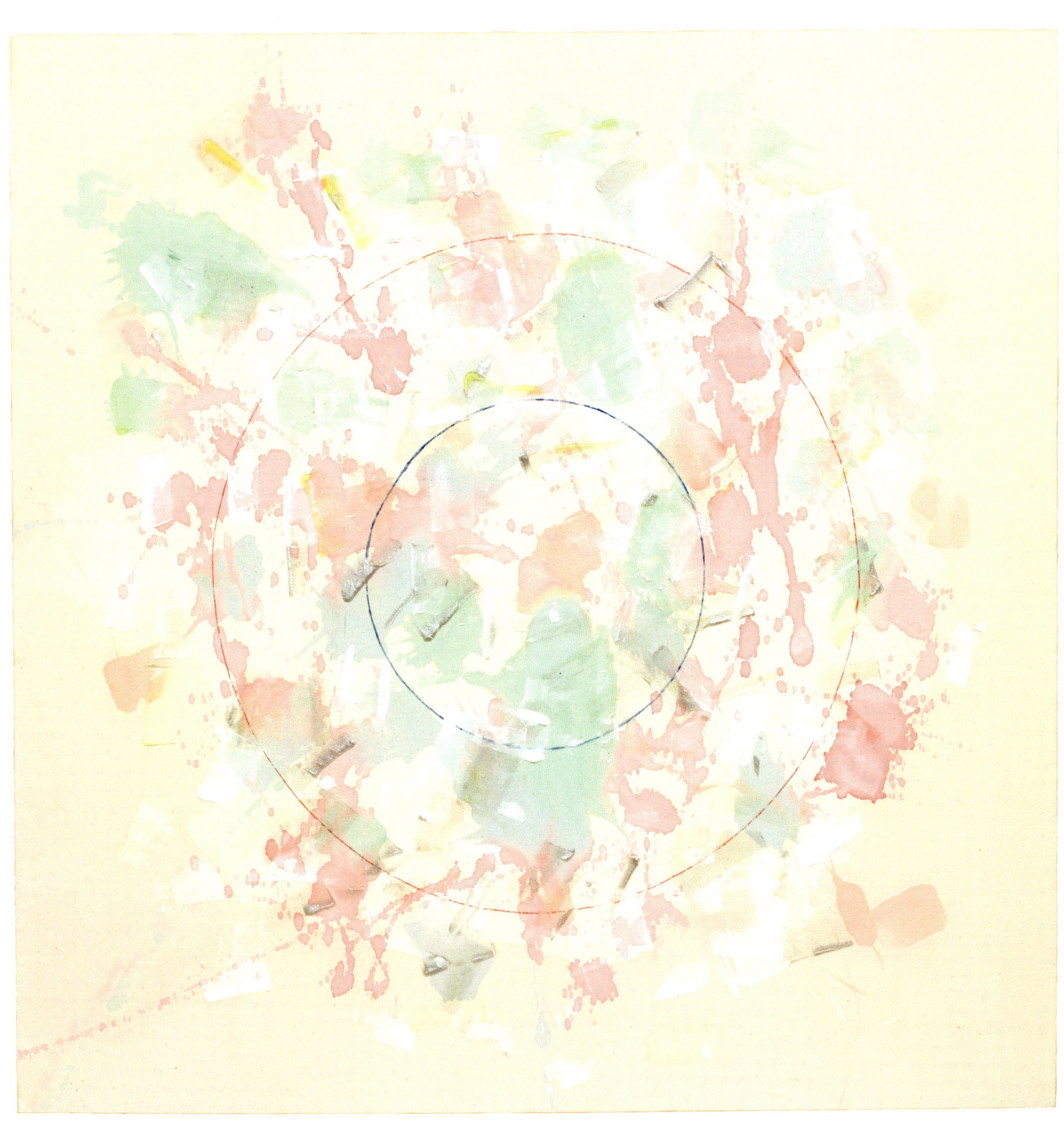

Into the Cool No. 19 2006 acrylic on canvas 63 3/16 x 63 3/16"

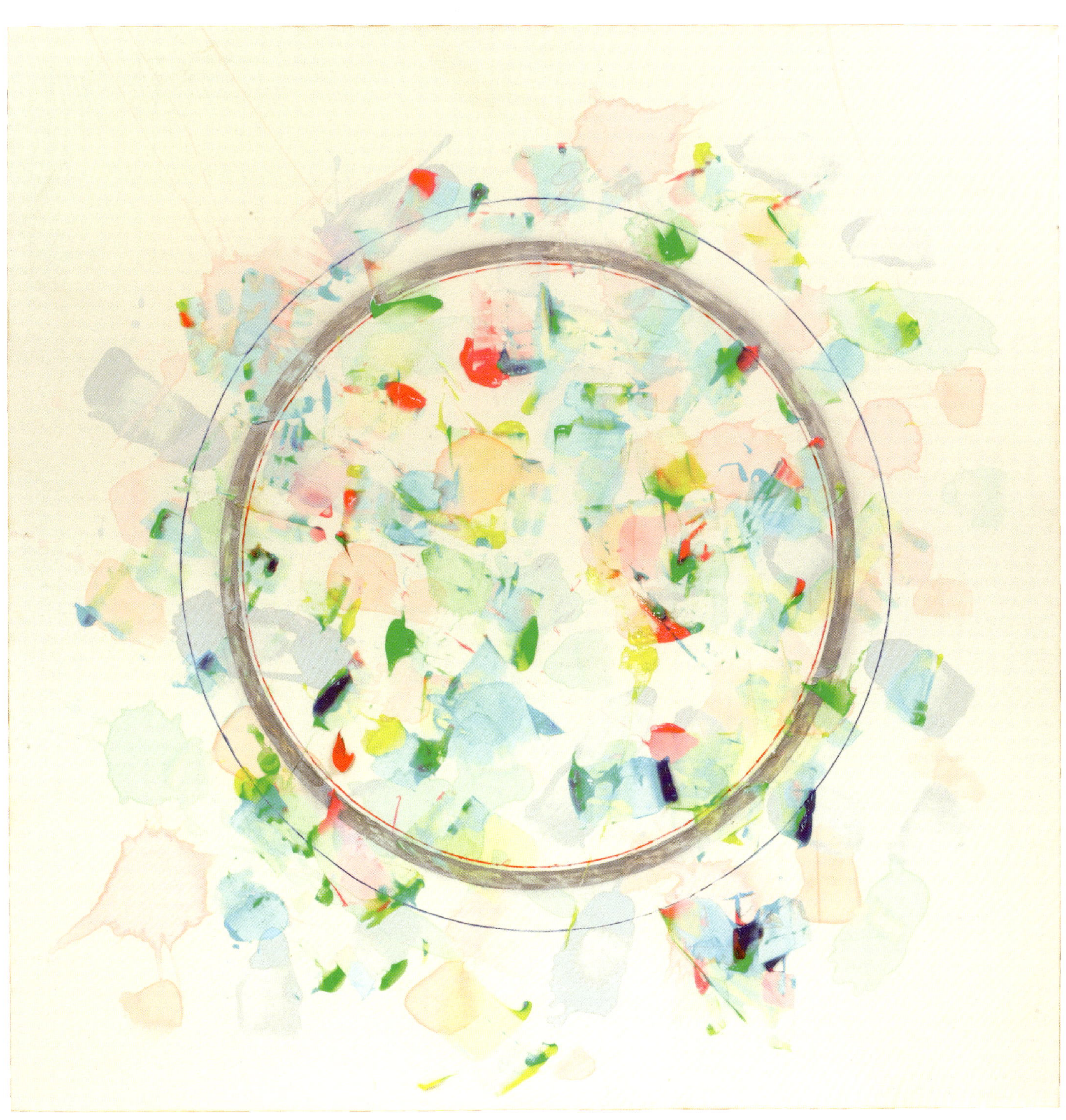

Burst 2006 acrylic on canvas 66 ¾ x 66 ¾"

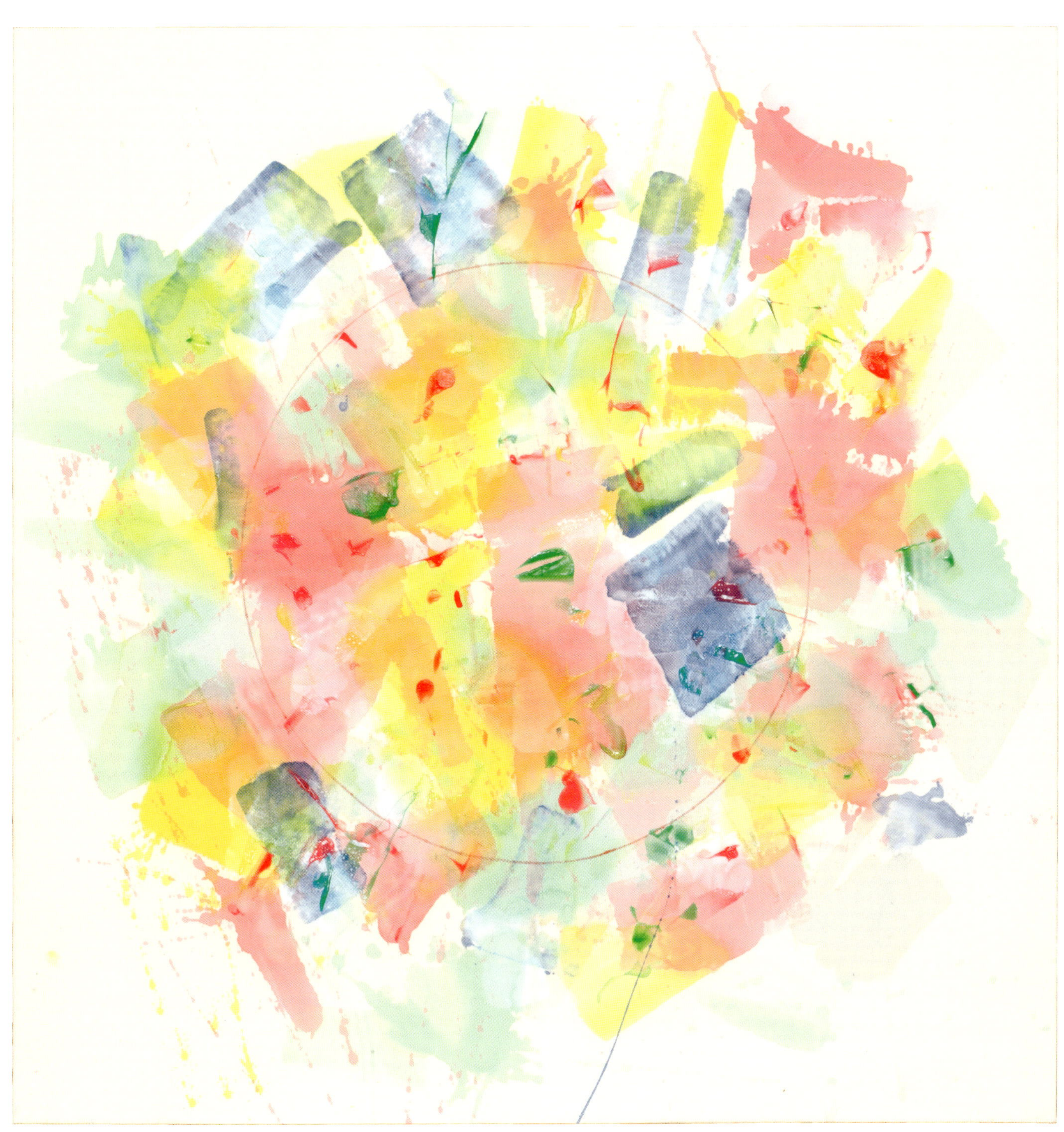

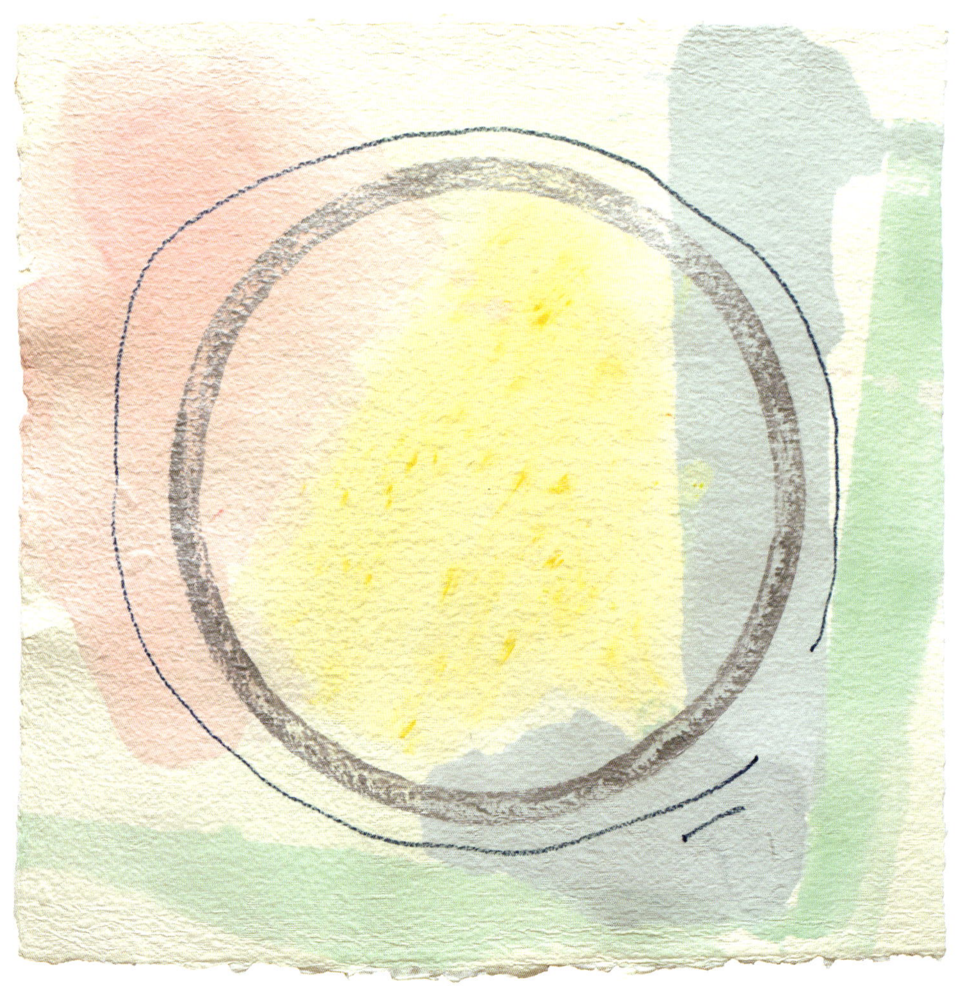

Untitled 2007 mixed medium and acrylic on handmade paper 23 ¼ x 23 ¼"

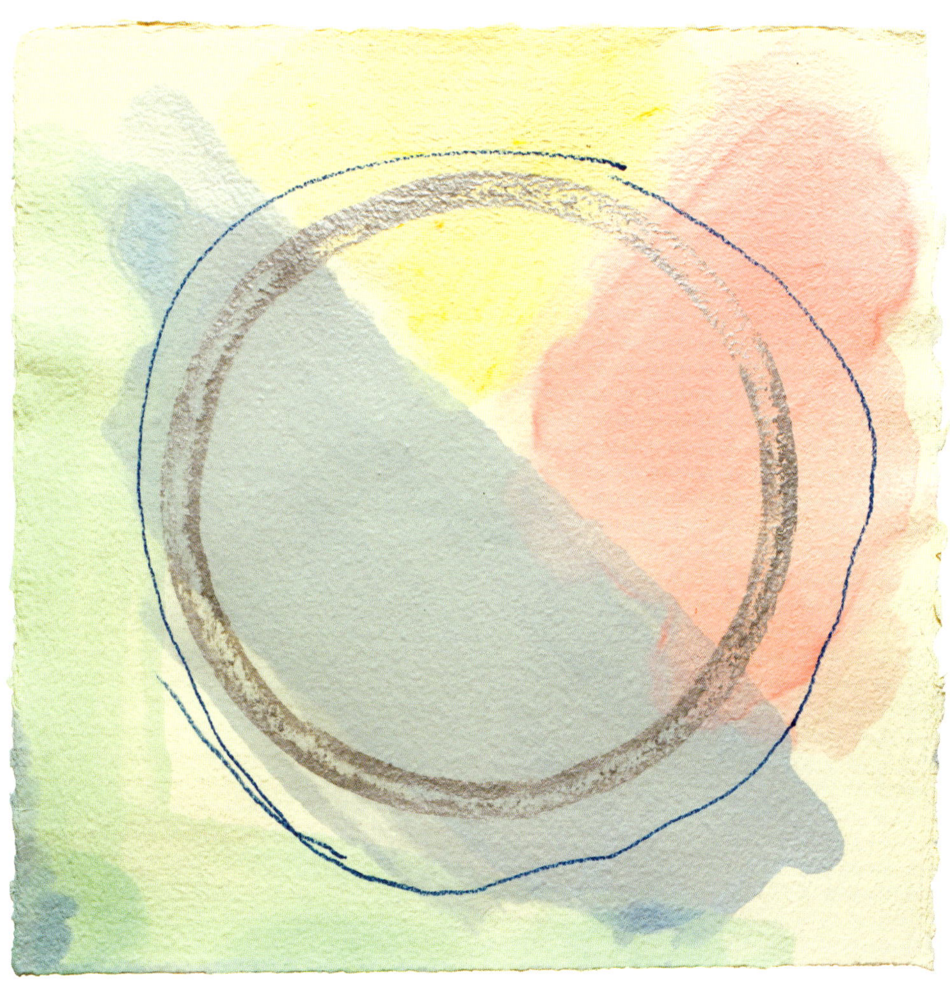

Untitled 2007 mixed medium and acrylic on handmade paper 23 ½ x 23 ½"

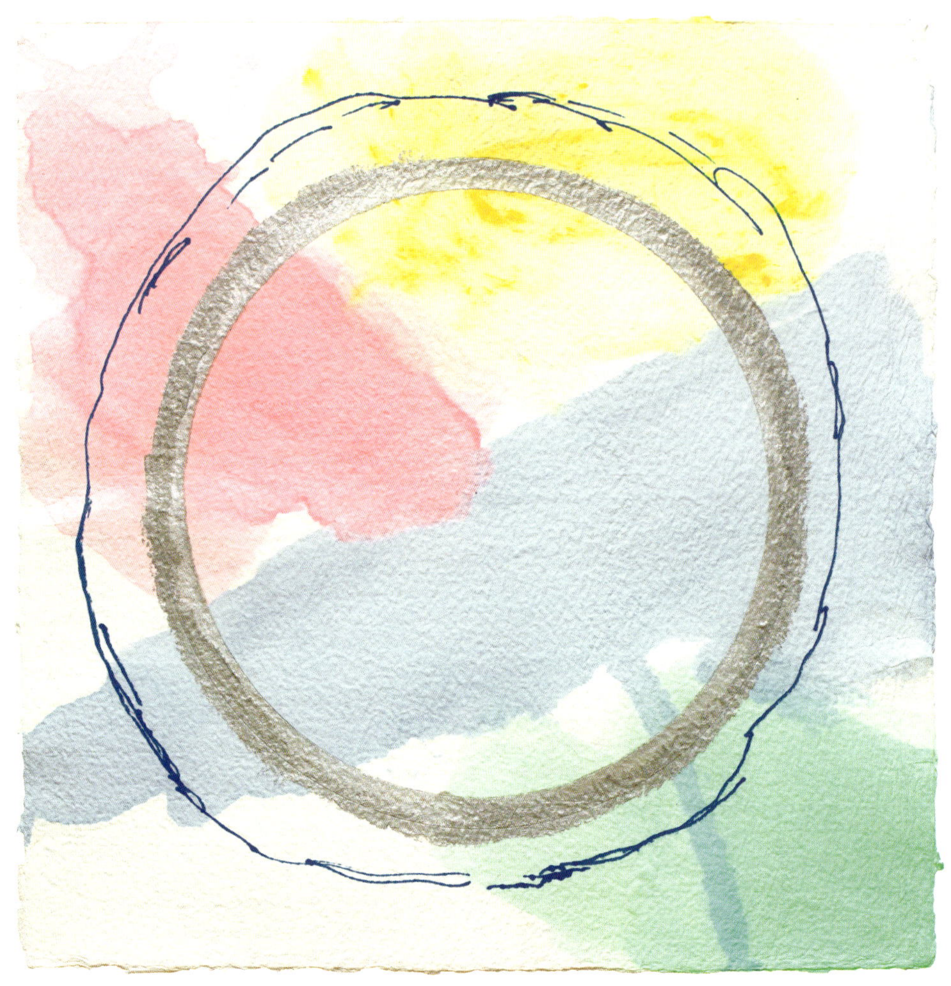

Untitled 2007 mixed medium and acrylic on handmade paper 22 ¾ x 22 ¾"

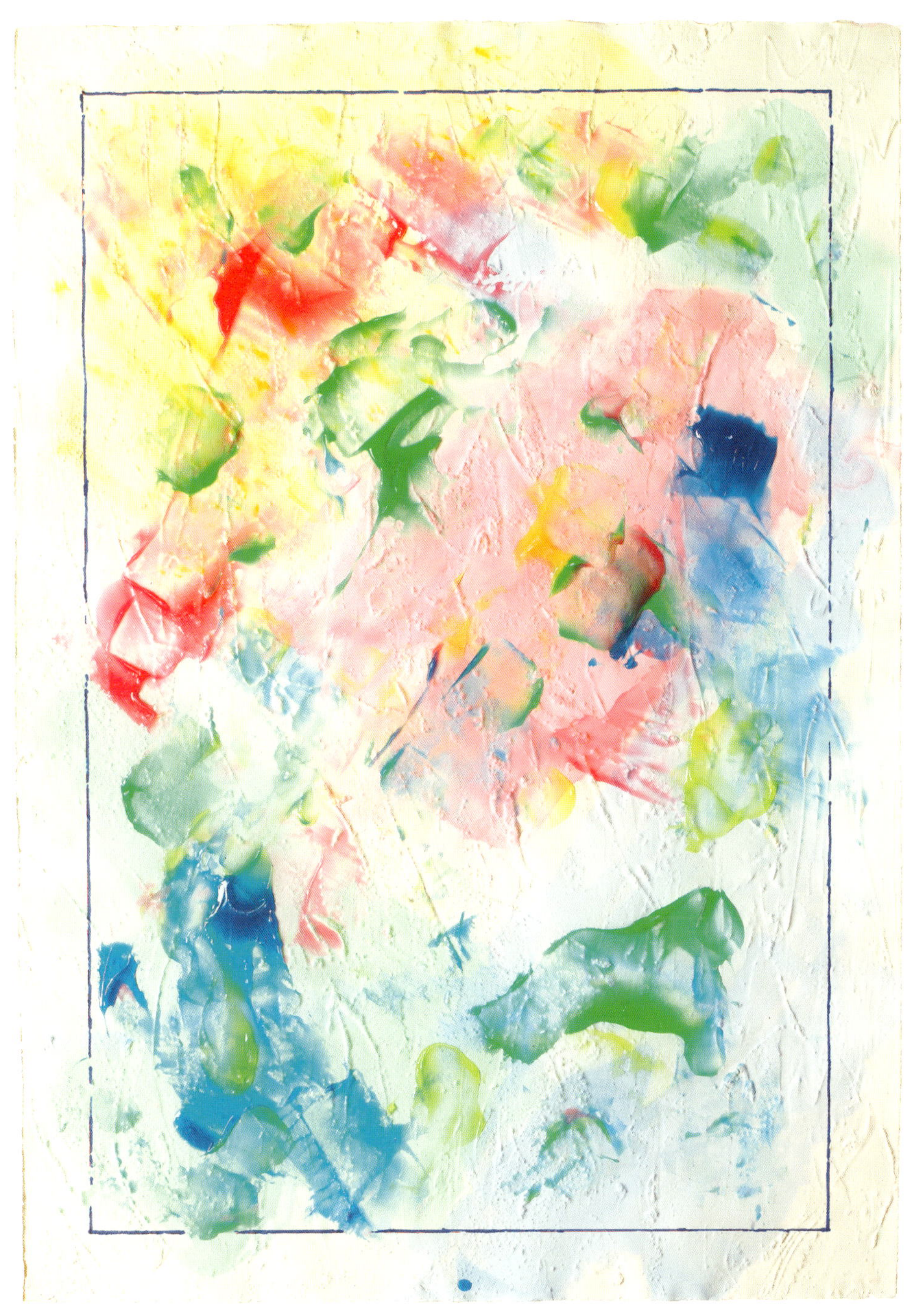

Untitled 2007 mixed medium and acrylic on handmade paper 41 ⅜ x 29 ⅜"

36	Into the Cool No. 15	2006	acrylic on canvas	62 x 62"
38	Into the Cool No. 16	2006	acrylic on canvas	55 x 55"
40	Into the Cool No. 17	2006	acrylic on canvas	60 x 60"
42	Into the Cool No. 18	2006	acrylic on canvas	62 x 62"
44	Into the Cool No. 19	2006	acrylic on canvas	63 3/16 x 63 3/16"
46	Burst	2006	acrylic on canvas	66 3/4 x 66 3/4"

48	Untitled	2007	mixed medium and acrylic on handmade paper	23 1/4 x 23 1/4"
49	Untitled	2007	mixed medium and acrylic on handmade paper	23 1/2 x 23 1/2"
50	Untitled	2007	mixed medium and acrylic on handmade paper	22 3/4 x 22 3/4"
51	Untitled	2007	mixed medium and acrylic on handmade paper	41 3/8 x 29 3/8"

Cover: *Into the Cool No. 4*, 2006 (detail)

Photography:
Tom Barratt and Kerry Ryan McFate; cover and pp. 12–33, 36–47
Kerry Ryan McFate; pp. 35, 48–51
Courtesy National Gallery of Art, Washington, D.C.; p. 9
Courtesy Kenneth Noland Studio and Archives; pp. 7–8
Allison V. Smith © Allison V. Smith; p. 4

Design: Tomo Makiura and Mine Suda

Color correction: Motohiko Tokuta

Production: Pace Gallery

Printing: Meridian Printing, East Greenwich, Rhode Island

Library of Congress Control Number: 2016962666
ISBN: 978-1-935410-90-4